ROGER BOULTON

Stewart House

TORONTO

TTC street-car

Union Station (1927)

Pearson International

(previous page) The Skydome and the CN Tower

Canadian Cataloguing in Publication Data

Boulton, Roger
  Toronto

(Canadian places series)
ISBN 0-7710-2650-1

1. Toronto (Ont.) – Description – Guide-books.
2. Toronto (Ont.) – Description – Views. I. Title.
II. Series

FC3097.18.B6 1990   917.13′541044   C90-093448-4
F1059.5.T683B6 1990

Design by Falcom Design and Communications Inc., Toronto
Produced by Boulton Publishing Services Inc., Toronto
Printed and bound in Hong Kong by Book Art Inc., Toronto

Any enthusiast tempted to say that "now Toronto truly has it all" might pause to think that by next week, if not tomorrow morning, Toronto will have added yet something more to offer in this range of attractions that multiply at such an astounding rate. From Old Fort York and the Scadding Cabin, earliest house that survives, to the 1,815-feet CN Tower, and its monumental mate, the Skydome, has been but a scant 200 years. In the past 20 of these Toronto has changed more radically than in all that went before.

Only a couple of decades ago this was still a quiet family town, with a very domestic character, an agreeable home if you didn't crave too much excitement. Now it is a vibrant metropolis, with a population of 70 cultures from all corners of the globe, and a cultural life that stops not day nor night throughout the year. More movies are made here than anywhere in North America except Los Angeles and New York. There is more theatre than anywhere else except New York and London. There are so many

Convention Centre escalators

restaurants now that it is impossible to count them. And so on and so on.

Toronto today is a welcome blend of old and new, of the familiar and the comfortable with the challenging and dynamic, all working well together at this time and in this uniquely stimulating place. Carefully restored Victorian terraces, wrought-iron facades, and warm old pioneer brick, perfect little gardens and a hundred parks, forested ravines and sand-girt islands, farmers markets and stately mansions, mingle together with high-tech towers and malls, with state-of-the-art entertainment centres, with imposing edifices of government and civic pride, with Canada's largest libraries and museums, with theatres, concert-halls and universities of international renown.

All this is depicted in the pages of this little book.

Here is Toronto's wealth of vitality, colour, variety, with the Lakeshore and the Islands, Harbourfront and High Park and Ontario Place, with the Caribbean festival of Caribana, and a celebration of all the different cultures at Caravan. Here are Fort York, the first schoolhouse (Enoch Turner's), the Campbell House, Mackenzie House, the Grange, Osgoode Hall, and the Queen's Park Parliament Buildings, the City Halls old and new, the Scarborough Civic Centre, the CN Tower and the Skydome and Ontario Place. Here are St Lawrence and Kensington Markets, Yorkville, "Honest Ed's", the Royal Ontario Museum, the Art Gallery, the Science Centre, the Eaton Centre, Roy Thomson Hall, and the racetracks, and the street cars, and Spadina, and Casa Loma, and the Scarborough Bluffs...

Ontario Place with HMCS Haida

Ontario Place

Ontario Place

Have we forgotten something? Perhaps, because there is so much to see. And Toronto still keeps growing and changing. What lies ahead? We can only say for certain that Toronto 2000 will have moved on as far again from Toronto now as today has come from twenty years ago. But we who live here intend to keep the quality that we have, with the feeling of a great place to visit and a captivating city in which to live.

Ontario Place with the Exhibition Stadium

Harbourfront

Old Fort York established 1793

William Lyon Mackenzie House (1837)

Kortright Conservation Centre

The Scadding Cabin

View from The Grange (1817)

Enoch Turner Schoolhouse (1848)

The Grange (1817)

St Lawrence Hall (1850)

The Gooderham and Worts Distillery Building

Campbell House (1822)

Casa Loma roofs, master bedroom, stables, and general view

Casa Loma (1914)

Centre Island

Historic lighthouse on Hanlan's Point

Toronto Island from the CN Tower

Centre Island Park

Island ferry

St Lawrence Market

Street vendor, Yorkville

Kensington Market

St Lawrence Market

Saturday morning, St Lawrence Market

Outdoor café, Yorkville

Hazelton Avenue

General view at night from the University area

Cinesphere, Ontario Place

A few of Toronto's many cultures

Niagara Street

Caribana festival

Ukrainian dancing at "Caravan"

Caribana festival

Outside the Skydome

Spanish dancing at "Caravan"

Queen's Park Provincial Parliament Buildings (1886–1892)   *Osgoode Hall (1857)*

Spadina House interior

Spadina House (1866)

Upper Canada College

Aerial looking north from Yonge and St Clair

Varsity Stadium, University of Toronto

University of Toronto, Victoria College

University of Toronto, Hart House, Soldiers Tower

University of Toronto, the Cloisters

University of Toronto, Robarts Library

University of Toronto, Philosopher's Walk

Ed Mirvish's store on Bloor West

Outside the "Royal Alex", with Ed's Warehouse

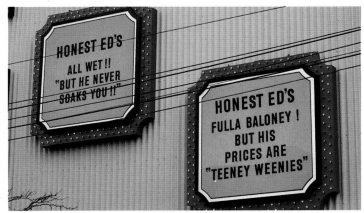

Outside "Honest Ed's"

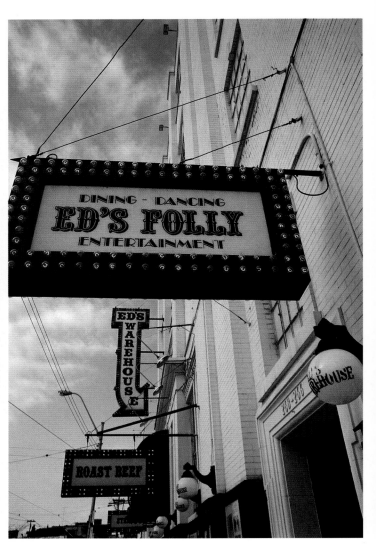

Ed's Folly

Gooderham ("Flatiron") Building (1892)

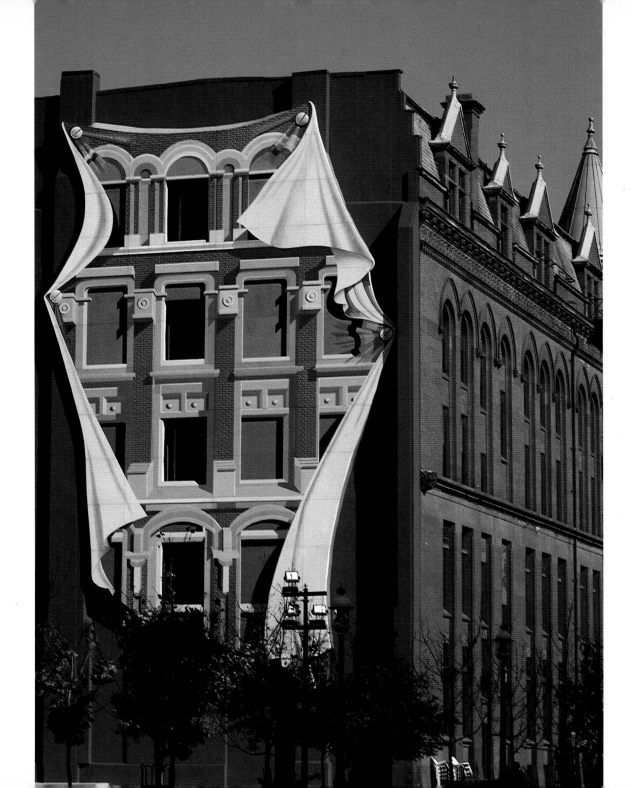

Woodbine Race Track

Morning workout, Greenwood track

Woodbine Race Track

Canadian National Exhibition

Roy Thomson Hall

The Eaton Centre

Skydome, opening the roof

Ontario Science Centre

Royal Ontario Museum

Ontario Science Centre

Art Gallery of Ontario

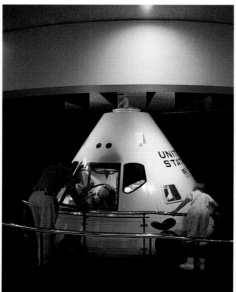

Old Bank of Montreal Building (1886)

Royal York Hotel

Scarborough Civic Centre

Royal Bank Tower

Freighters in harbour

Views along the Gardiner Expressway

Toronto harbour

Old City Hall (1899)

Nathan Phillips Square

*Nathan Phillips Square and
the City Hall (1965)*

*Skating on the pool in winter,
Nathan Phillips Square*

Ontario Hydro Building

Windsurfing off Ashbridge Bay Park

Kew Beach Park

Moon over the harbourfront

Scarborough Bluffs

Bluffer's Park from the air

Bluffer's Park, Scarborough

Downtown and the CN Tower looking east at sunrise from Humberside Park

Royal Bank Tower at dawn

Toronto harbour looking west